C0-BKF-070

EARTH'S ROCKY PAST

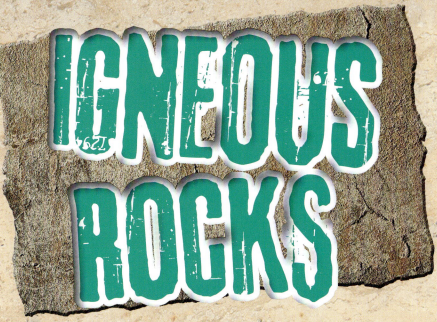

IGNEOUS ROCKS

Richard Spilsbury

PowerKiDS press
New York

Published in 2016 by **The Rosen Publishing Group**
29 East 21st Street, New York, NY 10010

Produced for Rosen by Calcium

Editors for Calcium: Sarah Eason and Harriet McGregor
Designers: Paul Myerscough and Jessica Moon
Illustrator: Venetia Dean

Picture credits: Cover: Dreamstime: David Williamson; Inside: Dreamstime: 13claudio13 11t,
Steve Allen 22–23, Fabrizio Argonauta 27, Alexey Astakhov 9c, Patrick Barry 4, Catwoman666
15b, Claffra 8, Ian Danbury 6–7t, Narongrit Dantragoon 15t, Jody Dingle 21, Freesurf69 17,
Vladislav Gajic 6–7b, Vladislav Gurfinkel 22b, Happystock 5b, Juliengrondin 26–27t, Junkgirl
13, Kacpura 19, Karol Kozlowski 24, Light & Magic Photography 25, Alessio Moiola 18–19,
Martin Novak 1, 8–9t, Les Palenik 26–27b, Pancaketom 23r, Iryna Rasko 5t, Thomasamm 11b,
Vulkanette 12, Wastesoul 20t; Shutterstock: severija 20b.

Cataloging-in-Publication Data
Spilsbury, Richard.
Igneous rocks / by Richard Spilsbury.
p. cm. — (Earth's rocky past)
Includes index.
ISBN 978-1-4994-0829-4 (pbk.)
ISBN 978-1-4994-0828-7 (6 pack)
ISBN 978-1-4994-0827-0 (library binding)
1. Igneous rocks — Juvenile literature.
I. Spilsbury, Richard, 1963-. II. Title.
QE461.S65 2016
552'.1—d23

Manufactured in the United States of America
CPSIA Compliance Information: Batch WS15PK: For Further Information contact Rosen Publishing, New York, New York at 1-800-237-9932

CONTENTS

IGNEOUS ROCKS

Have you ever seen hot wax run down the side of a candle and set hard as it cools? Well, one of the three main types of rocks that make up our Earth's surface forms in the exact same way, but from molten rock called **magma**.

Magma at Earth's surface is called **lava**.

RUNNY ROCK

Magma forms when rock melts deep underground. That is because the temperatures and **pressures** there are much higher than those at Earth's surface. It is hotter underground because it is nearer to the hottest part of our planet, which is the center, or **core**, of the Earth. The pressure is much higher because of the downward push of millions of tons of rock above.

FORMING ROCK

The word "igneous" means "formed through fire." **Igneous rock** forms from magma. **Volcanoes** are cracks in the Earth's **crust** (outer layer). Inside volcanoes is

4

red-hot, liquid magma. When volcanoes **erupt**, magma reaches Earth's surface. At the surface, magma is called lava. It cools quickly and hardens into new igneous rock. However, when magma rises through gaps that do not reach the surface, this magma cools more slowly. It forms other igneous rocks underground in Earth's crust.

granite statue

Clues to the Past

Some igneous rock, such as granite, has large grains, or pieces, inside. Others, such as basalt, have tiny grains. This is a clue to how they formed. Large grains need longer to form, so they formed while the magma was slowly cooling underground. Basalt has tiny grains because it formed from fast-cooling lava.

ROCK STAR STORIES

In 2013, a new island called Niijima appeared in the sea off the coast of Japan. This new igneous rock formed due to the eruption of a deep-sea volcano. By 2014, Niijima had grown enough to join up with another nearby island!

granite mountain

ROCKS FROM BENEATH

One of the simplest differences between igneous rocks is whether they formed at the surface or underground. Those that formed underground are called intrusive. That is because the magma intruded, or pushed, into rock above it.

This granite tor (rock formation) is an intrusive igneous formation.

RISING UP

Magma can reach temperatures of around 1,800° F (1,000° C). It rises into holes and cracks in rock above it, in a similar way to a hot-air balloon rising through the surrounding cooler air. Once the magma can rise no farther, it starts to cool. It cools slowly, over thousands or millions of years. This is because the rocks that surround the magma deep underground are still much hotter than those at the surface.

MINERALS AND CRYSTALS

All rocks are made from one or more **minerals**. In a rock, the minerals are solid. However, in magma, they have melted and stuck together. When magma cools, the different minerals in it each start to form solid, regular-shaped pieces called **crystals**. The crystals grow bigger and bigger as more magma slowly cools down around them. Granite is one of the most common intrusive rocks. It is usually made up of crystals of clear quartz, white or pink feldspar, and dark brown biotite minerals.

Clues to the Past

Some mountains that tower over the land today are made from intrusive igneous rock that formed underground long ago. Over thousands or millions of years, the softer rock above them was gradually **weathered** by chemicals in rainwater or by temperature changes. The weathered pieces of soft rock were **eroded** by moving water and wind. This left the harder igneous rock standing as it weathers more slowly.

intrusive igneous mountain

BIRTH OF GEMSTONES

The most valuable and biggest gemstones on Earth are often found in the jewelry of rich, famous, or royal people. Many gemstones were made when igneous rocks formed underground.

quartz

CHANGING MAGMA

Gemstones mostly form because of changes in intrusive magma as it cools and turns into igneous rock. Most magma contains water. This water has **dissolved** chemicals, like silica, within it. It also contains unusual **elements**, including beryllium and boron. The last section of magma to harden contains a lot of this mineral-rich water. Large crystals or gemstones, like emeralds and tourmaline, form in this magma.

These emeralds formed in gaps in cooling magma, which is now igneous rock.

GROWING IN GAPS

Gemstones sometimes form in bubbles in magma. As the magma cools, mineral-rich water collects there. It gradually turns into crystals of minerals like rubies and topaz. Gemstones also form in cracks in cooling igneous rock. Water from the surface trickles underground. There, it warms up and dissolves minerals from magma, creating lines or **veins** of crystals.

SURFACING ROCKS

If you squeeze a tube of toothpaste, it spurts out of the top. Great pressures underground push lava out of the Earth's surface in the same way. This forms **extrusive** rocks.

REACHING THE SURFACE

Magma rises in natural gaps between **plates** (pieces) of the Earth's crust. The crust is a little like a cracked eggshell on a hard-boiled egg, where pieces of shell can be pressed together or pulled apart. In places where plates are pulled apart, rock is thinner and the magma can melt a path through the thin rock to the surface.

AT EARTH'S SURFACE

At the Earth's surface, minerals in the lava quickly become harder. They form very small crystals in the rock. Most extrusive rock is a black rock called basalt. On land, the top layer of lava cools first over the runnier lava beneath, a lot like the wrinkly skin on cooling custard! Ropy lavas are igneous rocks that resemble ropes because the wrinkles have turned to stone.

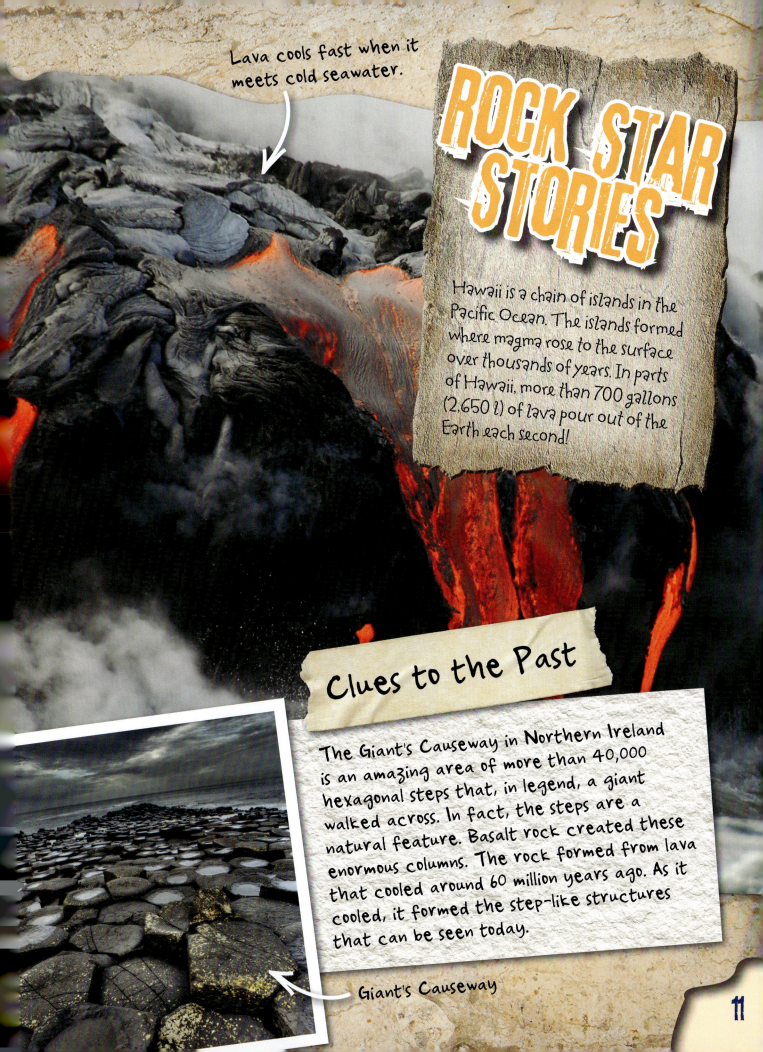

Lava cools fast when it meets cold seawater.

ROCK STAR STORIES

Hawaii is a chain of islands in the Pacific Ocean. The islands formed where magma rose to the surface over thousands of years. In parts of Hawaii, more than 700 gallons (2,650 l) of lava pour out of the Earth each second!

Clues to the Past

The Giant's Causeway in Northern Ireland is an amazing area of more than 40,000 hexagonal steps that, in legend, a giant walked across. In fact, the steps are a natural feature. Basalt rock created these enormous columns. The rock formed from lava that cooled around 60 million years ago. As it cooled, it formed the step-like structures that can be seen today.

Giant's Causeway

VIOLENT VOLCANOES!

Many extrusive rocks form where volcanoes explode. A volcano is a **vent** (hole) in the Earth's crust that reaches down to a **reservoir** of magma many miles underground.

volcanic eruption at night

EXPLODING VOLCANOES

The magma from a reservoir under a volcano does not trickle out of a vent all the time. The magma that rises to the top hardens and blocks the top of the vent. As more magma and gases rise toward the top of the sealed vent, they push against the surface. In some volcanoes, the pressure builds up so much that the magma suddenly breaks through the surface and there is an eruption.

CONES AND SHIELDS

Volcanoes have different shapes depending on the types of lava that they contain. Cone volcanoes have tall, steep-sided mountainsides. They form from layers of rock that pile high around the vent after sticky lava eruptions. Shield volcanoes are shaped like flattened hills. They form when runny lava spreads out quickly, and forms smaller structures.

Clues to the Past

At Yellowstone National Park scientists noticed that a large area of land had risen 28.5 inches (72 cm) since 1923. They figured out that there must be an ancient volcano deep underground. Rising magma is pushing the land upward below a blocked vent.

ROCK STAR STORIES

The largest volcanic eruption in history happened at Krakatau, Indonesia, on August 27, 1883. It was so powerful that the blast destroyed two-thirds of the island. The blast could be heard more than 2,800 miles (4,500 km) away in Australia. Since then, the volcano has grown again, and many scientists think it is due for another huge eruption.

cone volcano

EXPLOSIVE ROCKS

The most explosive eruptions in the natural world happen when volcanoes are heavily blocked with very sticky magma. Pressure builds up behind the block. Eventually, the pressure becomes too much as the volcano explodes. The lava flows shoot out and form some of the world's most amazing igneous rocks.

SHOOTING BOMBS

Eruptions shatter the solid rock blocking the vent into jagged pieces that fly into the air. These chunks fall and can stick together, along with lava or fallen **ash**, to make a type of rock called breccia. Strange football-shaped rocks near an eruption site are volcanic bombs. These formed when lava blobs shot upward and then fell back down to Earth.

SUPER-LIGHT ROCKS

Sometimes the force of the hot gases shooting from a volcano can turn magma into lightweight and unusual rocks. Lava can explode into tiny pieces that cool and fall to Earth as ash. When ash builds up and hardens, it forms a rock called tuff. Small blobs of silica-rich lava fly into the air and cool very rapidly. They solidify (become solid) and fall to Earth as hard droplets or even thin hairs of natural glass called obsidian.

pumice

On some coastlines around the world, the waves bring in pieces of white or gray rock that float on the water. Pumice floats because it contains bubbles of volcanic gases. The bubbles became trapped inside the rock when it formed. Finding pumice in floating pieces, or in layers under the soil, proves there was once a volcanic eruption nearby.

ROCK STAR STORIES

Mount St. Helens is a volcano. It was **dormant** (inactive) for 120 years before it erupted in 1980. The explosive eruption sent a cloud of ash 13 miles (21 km) into the sky. At ground level, millions of tons of red-hot ash and gases shot down the side of the mountain. They cleared thousands of trees and covered roads and villages.

Gray ash and small rocks cover Mount St. Helens.

IGNEOUS WORLD

Our planet's crust is mostly made from igneous rock. Much of this is buried underground beneath another rock called **sedimentary rock**. This is rock that has formed from pieces of weathered and eroded rock, like igneous rock.

TOWERING MOUNTAINS

Enormous chunks of intrusive rocks form most of the world's mountain ranges. Igneous rock is very hard and is not easily weathered. It also remains **intact** during major movements such as stretching of the Earth's crust. Mountain ranges also form as plates shift and shove up rocks that may have been beneath the surface before the shift. One example is the Sierra Nevada Mountains, in the western United States, with its famous peaks including Half Dome and El Capitan.

AMAZING LAVA FIELDS

The Chaine des Puys, in France, is an area of more than 50 dormant volcanoes. Most of these volcanoes were formed during a single eruption. In other parts of the world, lava erupts from many cracks in Earth's crust rather than from individual vents. The spread of lava has created flat **plateaus** of igneous rock, like the Deccan Trap, part of the Deccan Plateau in India, which covers 190,000 square miles (500,000 sq km). That is an area bigger than the whole of California!

ROCK STAR STORIES

More than half of the world's volcanoes are found around the edge of the Pacific Ocean, in an area called the Ring of Fire. This is where the enormous plate that lies under the Pacific Ocean meets six other plates. Around the Ring of Fire, magma constantly reaches or nears the surface. The Ring is also where most of Earth's earthquakes happen. An earthquake is the shaking of the ground caused when plates push into, rub against, and slide past each other.

eroded igneous rocks in the Seychelles, near Africa

GETTING IGNEOUS ROCKS

People use igneous rock as a **resource**. People mine for the rocks they need. Sometimes intrusive rock is revealed following weathering and **erosion**. New extrusive rock is found at the surface of volcano sites.

BLASTING AND DIGGING

Intrusive igneous rocks with large crystal structures are very hard. People often use explosives to mine these rocks from **quarries**. They drill vertical holes at the top of a cliff face and set explosives in them. By exploding all the holes at the same time they can make a large chunk of rock fall off the cliff face. Volcanic rocks with smaller grains are slightly softer, so people can cut and break off pieces using powerful diggers.

Clues to the Past

In some places, like Dartmoor, in the UK, there are blocks of igneous rocks that are full of drill holes. These blocks are the remains of mining activities that took place before powerful mining machinery existed. People drilled holes into the rock by hand and then hammered iron chisels between them to split it. It was backbreaking work.

diamond in kimberlite rock

granite quarry

ROCKY CLUES

People often search for igneous rocks because they give clues about the location of valuable materials, including gemstones and **ores**. Ores are concentrated amounts of metal minerals, like copper and gold. They are often found as veins within igneous rocks. For example, **geologists** search for kimberlite rock because they know that by digging down into it or sifting through eroded stones from it they may locate diamonds!

TOUGH ROCKS

Some igneous rocks are amongst the toughest rocks on the planet. This makes them ideal for use as strong and **durable** materials. The toughest ones include intrusive granite and gabbro, and extrusive basalt.

GORGEOUS GRANITE

Granite is often used for polished decorative surfaces, ranging from countertops and stonework on buildings to headstones. Polishing reveals the rock's beautiful crystal structure. Granite withstands normal weathering for a long time so it stays tough and continues to look good. However, after very long periods, weathered granite crumbles as the crystals come apart.

Cages of tough igneous rock prevent sea erosion.

variety of beautiful granite patterns

STRONG STONE

Granite, gabbro, and basalt are all broken into pieces and crushed to use in supporting roles. For example, crushed stone is used to support railroads and made into **asphalt** used to build roads. Larger chunks are piled up along coasts to prevent sea erosion. These rocks are heavy and strong, so they stay in place and endure great forces without moving.

Clues to the Past

Most of the sand on beaches worldwide is made from tiny grains of quartz that were once inside granite. Over thousands of years, the feldspar and mica minerals in granite weathered and eroded into clay, but the tougher quartz remained in larger pieces. Rivers and oceans carried the sand away, then **deposited**, or dumped it, on beaches.

ROCK STAR STORIES

Mt. Rushmore

One of the most famous granite sculptures in the United States is that of the four US presidents at Mt. Rushmore, South Dakota. The heads were carved into the cliff between 1927 and 1941 by Gutzon and Lincoln Borglum. The artists planned to sculpt the presidents' upper bodies, too, but ran out of money to complete the project.

VERSATILE VOLCANICS

Did you know that some igneous rocks are used to make faded blue jeans and knife blades? Volcanic extrusive rocks are rarely as tough as intrusives, but they are very **versatile**.

ROCK RUBBING

Pumice is widely used as a gentle **abrasive**. Some people rub pumice on their feet to make hard skin smooth. New blue jeans are washed with pumice lumps to give them a worn appearance. Most pumice is used because it can be ground into a powder, then mixed with cement and made into light concrete blocks used for building.

Clues to the Past

Gold sheen obsidian is black or brown with tiny golden streaks or dots. When viewed through a microscope, it is clear that the streaks or dots are lines of tiny bubbles. The bubbles were made by hot steam from a volcano, and then trapped inside the rock when the obsidian formed.

sheen obsidian

ROCK STAR STORIES

moais, Easter Island

On a tiny volcanic island in the middle of the Pacific Ocean stand more than 800 human-like statues. The statues are between 6 and 30 feet (2 and 9 m) tall and have giant heads. They are called the Easter Island statues, or moais. The statues were carved from **tuff** more than 500 years ago by the island's local people, the Rapa Nui. Some of the statues even had white coral eyes with obsidian pupils.

NATURAL GLASS

Obsidian often looks like shiny black glass but can also be reddish-brown, green, or have gold or silver sheens. This rock has no visible crystals and it can be broken along smooth, curved lines like regular glass. Broken edges can be as sharp as razors, and in the past obsidian was used to make knives and arrowheads. Obsidian blades are still sometimes used today for surgery, but are more often made into gemstones for jewelry.

ancient obsidian knife

LIVING BY VOLCANOES

Life near volcanoes can be good and bad. Volcanoes bring useful minerals to Earth's surface and volcanic heat provides people with an energy source. However, eruptions can be very dangerous.

VOLCANIC SOIL

Rock formed by volcanoes is rich in minerals from deep in Earth's crust. Over time, these weather to become part of soils around volcanoes. The minerals help crops grow large, strong, and produce a lot of fruit or vegetables. For example, some of Italy's best tomatoes, grapes, and vegetables grow in the dark volcanic soils from past eruptions of Mt. Etna.

POWER BENEATH

Near volcanoes the crust is often thin enough for magma to come to the surface. It heats surface water that trickles underground, causing hot springs and **geysers** to form.

vegetables growing on the slopes of a volcano

Geothermal power stations use volcanic heat to help make electricity.

People use the heat from springs and geysers for energy. They also pump water deep underground to heat it up and use the very hot water to make electricity, or to warm buildings, greenhouses, and swimming pools.

DANGER ZONES

There are around 1,300 active volcanoes worldwide, which means they have erupted in recent history. Eruptions can be fast and deadly if hot gases, ash, and bombs shoot from them. Even the slowest lava flows can knock down and burn everything in their path. Scientists carefully monitor active volcanoes. They also work closely with governments to keep people safe.

North Island, New Zealand, is famous for its volcanic landscapes but also for its farms. The island is green and lush owing to its rich, deep volcanic soil. The soil formed from volcanic ash that was weathered by the island's warm temperatures and plentiful rain. The area is famous as the heart of New Zealand's dairy industry, and many kiwifruits eaten worldwide come from there.

ROCK STAR STORIES

INCREDIBLE IGNEOUS

Igneous rocks are incredible because they are the only rocks we can actually see being formed when volcanoes erupt. Other igneous rocks are formed deep underground, but we can study how they have formed when intrusive rocks come to the Earth's surface.

Magma creates new rock all the time.

metamorphic rock

THE ROCK CYCLE

Pieces of weathered and eroded igneous rock can form layers and become new sedimentary rock. Sometimes sedimentary and igneous rock are pressed and heated when one plate dips beneath another. Then they form a third type of rock called **metamorphic rock**. When any rock is buried deep enough it becomes part of the magma that can then form new igneous rock. This constant recycling of rock into different forms is called the **rock cycle**. Igneous rocks are an important part of the rock cycle.

WINDOWS INTO OUR PLANET

Igneous rocks are a direct link to the incredible world inside Earth. For example, elements in some minerals gradually change over time, at a regular rate. Scientists can measure the elements in minerals to figure out the age of rocks. This is easiest in igneous rocks because all the crystals in them are the same age and formed from the same magma. Unlike igneous rocks, sedimentary and metamorphic rocks contain minerals with different ages.

ROCK STAR STORIES

In 2014, US scientists measured the age of a tiny crystal of sand from Australia. It formed 4.37 billion years ago, making it the oldest rock ever found. This fragment of igneous rock formed only a few hundred million years after the Earth itself first formed. It proves that even at the very beginning of our planet's life, it had a crust. Imagine that: a grain of sand can tell us something about the history of our world!

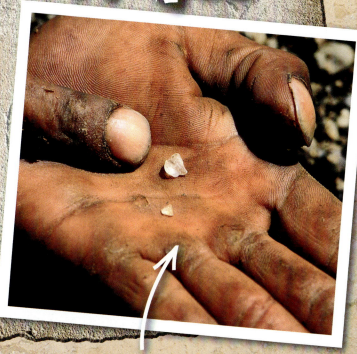

Igneous crystals are clues to the past.

ROCK YOUR WORLD!

Igneous rock can take a long time to form, but you can mimic the process using paper, glue, and water!

- two sheets of different colored construction paper
- food blender
- two cups of water
- one teaspoon of white glue
- adult helper
- strainer large enough to fit across the bowl
- large, deep bowl
- 12 sheets of newspaper

COMPLETE THESE STEPS:

1. First, tear the sheets of construction paper into small pieces.

2. Drop the pieces of paper into the blender. Carefully pour the water and glue into the blender.

3. Ask your adult to put the lid on the blender and turn it on. Keep it on until the paper and water are completely mixed together. You should be left with a thick, wet mash.

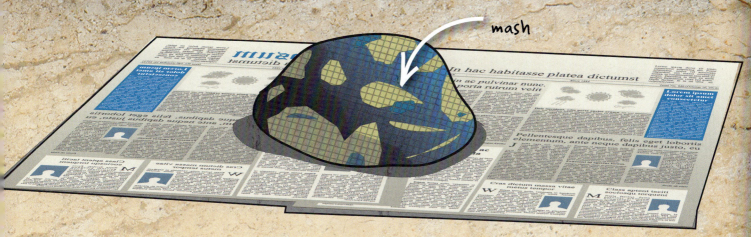
mash

4. Rest the strainer over the top of the bowl and pour the mash into the strainer. Leave the strainer over the bowl for about a half hour, so the water from the mash can drip through it.

5. Fold the newspaper sheets in half and lay them on the table. Squeeze the lump of mash while it is in the strainer and then put it on top of the newspaper. Leave this to dry and harden for at least three days.

WHAT HAPPENED?

When your papery mash dries, it should form a hard, lumpy "rock." Imagine that mixing the two different-colored paper pieces and water was like the melting of different rocks beneath the surface of the Earth. Your mash was like the molten rock we call magma. When magma cools and hardens it forms igneous rock. As your mash dried and hardened it formed a hard solid, too.

TRY IT OUT!

You can use paper and glue to mimic how sedimentary rock forms, too. Make two separate quantities of mash, one from blue paper and the other from yellow. While still damp, take half of each and flatten them on newspaper. Stack the alternate layers up and leave it to dry. Sedimentary rock has layers just like this!

GLOSSARY

abrasive Something that can grind, polish, or clean a hard surface.

ash The powder left after something has been completely burned.

asphalt Material used for road surfaces.

core Center of the Earth.

crust Hard, rocky layer on the surface of the Earth.

crystals Solids made up of regular, repeating patterns of particles.

deposited Put or set down.

dissolved Completely mixed with a liquid.

dormant Temporarily inactive.

durable Hard wearing.

elements Simplest chemical substances, like iron, carbon, or oxygen.

eroded Worn away.

erosion When soil and rock are carried away by water, ice, or wind.

erupt When a volcano explodes and hot, molten rock called lava spurts out of it.

extrusive Igneous rocks formed from lava above the Earth's surface.

geologists Scientists who study rocks and minerals.

geysers Holes in the ground that shoot out hot water and steam.

igneous rock Rock formed when magma cools and hardens.

intact Complete

intrusive Describes igneous rocks formed from magma deep within the Earth.

lava The name for magma when it emerges above Earth's surface.

magma Molten rock beneath Earth's crust.

metamorphic rock Rock changed from its original form by heat and/or pressure.

minerals Solid, naturally occurring substances that make up rocks, soil, and many other materials.

ores Naturally occurring rocks from which a metal or valuable mineral can be extracted.

plateaus Areas of level, high ground.

plates Giant pieces of rock that lie on the hot, molten rock in the center of Earth.

pressures Pushing forces when a weight is pressing down on something.

quarries Large holes in the ground where people dig for useful rocks or metals.

reservoir A large lake.

resource Thing that people can use.

rock cycle The constant formation, destruction, and recycling of rocks through Earth's crust.

sedimentary rock Rock made when tiny pieces of sediment are changed by heat and pressure into rock.

tuff Type of rock made from volcanic ash.

veins Narrow sections of minerals filling a gap in surrounding rock.

vent An opening in Earth's crust through which hot gases, water, or magma escape.

versatile Able to do many different things.

volcanoes Openings in Earth's surface where magma escapes from underground.

weathered When rock is broken down into small pieces by natural processes.